D0401205

Divorced:
Surviving the Pain

Divorced

MEDITATIONS ON DIVORCE

Surviving the Pain

Alice Stolper Peppler

CONCORDIA

PUBLISHING HOUSE

BT
707
.P46
1993

Originally published as *Divorced and Christian,* © 1974 Concordia Publishing House, St. Louis, MO. Revised 1993.

Scripture taken from the HOLY BIBLE, NEW INTERNATIONAL VERSION®. Copyright © 1973, 1978, 1984 by International Bible Society. Used by permission of Zondervan Publishing House. All rights resrved.

The "NIV" and "New International Version" trademarks are registered in the United States Patent and Trademark Office by International Bible Society. Use of either trademark requires the permission of International Bible Society.

Copyright © 1974, 1993 Concordia Publishing House
3558 S. Jefferson Avenue, St. Louis, MO 63118-3968
Manufactured in the United States of America

All rights reserved. No part of this publication may be reproduced, stored in a retrieval system, or transmitted, in any form or by any means, electronic, mechanical, photocopying, recording, or otherwise, without the prior written permission of Concordia Publishing House.

Library of Congress Cataloging-in-Publication Data

Peppler, Alice Stolper.
    Divorced : surviving the pain : meditations on divorce / Alice Stolper Peppler.
    Rev. ed of : Divorced and Christian. 1974.
    ISBN 0-570-04613-0
    1. Divorce—Religious aspects—Christianity. 2. Divorced women—Religious life. I. Peppler, Alice Stolper. Divorced and Christian. II. Title.
BT707.P46   1993
248.8'46—dc20   93-22209

1 2 3 4 5 6 7 8 9 10   02 01 00 99 98 97 96 95 94 93

To women
everywhere
suffering a loss

CONCORDIA COLLEGE LIBRARY
2811 NE HOLMAN ST.
PORTLAND, OR 97211-6099

Contents

Foreword

Even in the lives of Christians,
most certainly in the lives of Christians ...

There can be times when all reason and logic vanish,
When Evil envelopes our lives,
When all is madness, or suffering, or emptiness,
     or despair,
When not only the box bottom breaks,
   but the side supports collapse,
When *what could never happen in our family does,*
When despairing depths of doom loom in the darkness,
And fish on shore flop frantically to find the familiar,
When pain persists ... pounding, pounding ...
And cancer cuts through every cell,
When all the persistent planning, training, and loving
     of a lifetime
   smash and shrivel into shattered junk. ...

Even in the lives of Christians,
most certainly in the lives of Christians ...

There are times when the pastor no longer can play
     the physician,
When family and friends can no longer heal,
When the patient can no longer digest oral pills
     and comforting couplets,
When faith has reached the fray of the rope,
   and sackcloth is no balm to the boil,
When no human can help ... and God seems love-dry,
When one repeats like a ruined record, "Why, Why,
     Just tell me why!"

And the answer is silence ... sustained, still ...
When God has walked away, as if in Gethsemane,
And one realizes for the first time
The hope less-nessss of Christ's screammm ...
    "My God, My God, Why Hast Thou
    Forsaken Me?"

Even in the lives of Christians,
most certainly in the lives of Christians ...

From far in the distance, from where God has walked,
    comes rumbling thunder ... resounding, sounding ...
"BE STILL AND KNOW THAT I AM GOD!
You Question My Love? I AM Love!"

And silence reigns and silence sustains

And then if one hears ... through one's tears,
And then if one's still ... and works His will,
And then if one stays ... to await His ways,

Then one WILL know,
    will know God's love,
    and receive His Spirit,
    and, perhaps, finally

        see

           why ...

        I will praise You, O Lord,
          with my whole heart ...
        Though I walk in the midst
          of trouble,
          You preserve my life ...
        The Lord will fulfill
          His purpose for me;
        Your love, O Lord, endures forever ...
          Psalm 138:1, 7–8

Chapter 1

Introduction to Divorce

How lovely is Your dwelling place,
*   O Lord Almighty!*
My soul yearns, even faints
*   for the courts of the Lord;*
My heart and my flesh cry out
*   for the living God.*
                    Psalm 84:1–2

It's all over. One final session in court, and a life together is over. If the marriage had ended in death (you muse), there would have been a funeral. Your friends would have been with you for the final service. Word and Sacrament would have been a comfort. Next Sunday there would have been prayers for the survivors. The grief could have been open and even proud. One need not apologize for death. But this is divorce . . . and divorce is completely and utterly without honor.

Now you are alone. No matter who is with you, you are alone. You have begun a life that is totally unlike anything you have ever lived. It is not merely going back to the single state; it is to a new state that you're going. You have left your settled, comfortable, married world and entered an unsettled, separate one—a "limbo" you'll never completely share or explain to your single, married, or widowed friends. You'll soon learn what all divorced know: that there is no way to "tell it like it is" to outsiders, that there is no vicarious experience for divorce.

You've never had any preparation for this new state . . . not really. You remember wondering what it's like to be a parent, a mother. You remember querying occupations. You remember a whole childhood of multidimensional training; but unless it was a reality in your home, you never asked what it's like to be divorced, and no one ever considered preparing you for it. It would have been negative and self-defeating, perhaps, to even admit its possibility. But now its reality is even more negative. And you're not prepared . . . not really. And your family and friends aren't prepared . . . not really.

It's eerie. It's unreal. All time has stopped. You thought hard labor had begun with that first contraction so long ago. You timed and considered every contraction over the months or years. You hoped the divorce would have been final—the delivery room. But there's no relief yet. You're still back at the hospital door. You've only begun. And it will not be an easy delivery.

You're all alone,
    but not really.
The Spirit . . . the Son . . . the Father . . .
    they're all there, too.

Really!

> *God is our refuge and strength,*
>   *an ever-present help in trouble.*
> *Therefore we will not fear,*
>   *though the earth give way*
>   *and the mountains fall*
>   *into the heart of the sea,*
> *though its waters roar and foam*
>   *and the mountains quake*
>   *with their surging.*
>   *Psalm 46:1–3*

Chapter 2

Shock, Despair

To You I call, O Lord my Rock;
 do not turn a deaf ear to me.
If You remain silent,
 I will be like those who have
  gone down to the pit.
Hear my cry for mercy
 as I call to You for help . . .
   Psalm 28:1

For my days vanish like smoke;
 my bones burn like glowing embers.
My heart is blighted and withered like grass;
 I forget to eat my food.
Because of my loud groaning
 I am reduced to skin and bones.
I am like a desert owl,
 like an owl among the ruins.
I lie awake; I have become
 like a bird alone on a roof.
   Psalm 102:3–7

The shock of the marriage death occurs long before the divorce decree. When you first suspected your marriage was ending, you wondered what was happening to you. You didn't feel joyous or tragic or free or despairing—you just didn't feel! You were in a twilight zone of shock and unreality—a nightmarish suspension from which you vaguely expected to awaken. You were expected to awaken. You were a stranger to yourself; your husband was still more an unknown; and nothing made sense. You cried for help as if from outer space, with no one "real" around to hear.

HELP!
Help

h
e
l
p

if
only

Senselessness may have hovered for some time, but eventually it gave way to a feeling of loss. There is grief in marriage-breaking. It is natural enough when one still loves, but it exists even when one doesn't. A union, however bad it is, cannot be dissolved without a feeling of loss.

If the loss is especially dear or too overpowering, you may react with despondency. Strength sapped and spirit crushed by the demon of despair, you will be conscious of evil forces all around you. They'll be grinning, these grim phantoms, just waiting for you to give up so they can begin their victory feast. You will know too well the psalmist's anguished cry from the depths of nothingness, from the pits of hopelessness. You will think of, and perhaps seriously consider, suicide. You will wish to escape ... to escape ... to escape ... but it will seem impossible.

Nowhere
is too
low.

Swirling ...
darker and deeper ...

Darkness
     everywhere

Brimful living goblet
of doom and horror

They drink and rejoice,
    and I
        hate myself . . .

Peter walks on the water
    above the mud,
but not alone,
    never alone . . .
impossible.

Nowhere
   is too
     low.

Even there
Thou art there.

You're in mud—the muddy mire of despair. If you were raised in the church, you may recall your childhood Christian training—the memorization of Bible passages and hymns, the warnings of Satan as the roaring lion, the assurance of God's love and comfort, the innocent firm trust of your confirmation day, the zeal of your forefathers tolling their faith in a new world.

Thoughts flash through your mind; but before they are complete, new observations appear. Everything runs together. Your brain hops from this to that. You can't concentrate. You can't get organized. You flounder. You debate with yourself. You understand only one thing: your confusion.

God is LO
VE and of course you have Christi
an upbringing and so
hate, horror, LO (?loco?) VE
encompasses all.

ComeuntoMeandIwillgiveyourest.
Memmmmmory   work
to withstand the RoaRRRRing li
on.

Once in confirmation
"be thou faithful unto death"
the endless rote—rote—rote . . .
Where is that Faith?
Crushhh
ed in confound
ed, confus
ing, conflict
ing? Fool(ish) and fu
tile, lame Luther
an, lamenting . . . lost . . .
GOD IS
(I have loved thee with an everlasting) LOVE
waitontheLord

WAIT

on the Lord

   Again and again you will tell yourself that God is with
you. And again and again you will wonder. Back and forth,
over and over, you'll thrash about in this net you find yourself
in. You will question almost everything you ever learned—
truth, honor, friends, church, and the faith of your fathers.
But you will not discount the reality of God's love. It is still
too soon to give in to doubt. You will tell Job's advisers who

sneer in the back of your mind to desist. The world can be questioned, but not yet God. You thrash . . . but you still hold onto the line. . . .

Out of the depths I cry
to You, O Lord;
O Lord, hear my voice.
Let Your ears be attentive
to my cry for mercy.
If You, O Lord, kept a record of sins,
O Lord, who could stand?
But with You there is forgiveness;
therefore You are feared.
I wait for the Lord, my soul waits,
and in His Word I put my hope.
Psalm 130:1–5

Chapter 3

Physical Reactions

Save me, O God, for the waters
   have come up to my neck.
I sink in the miry depths, where there
   is no foothold.
I am come into the deep waters;
   the floods engulf me.
I am worn out calling for help;
   my throat is parched.
My eyes fail,
   looking for my God.
   Psalm 69:1–3

There will have been tears before the divorce—there will be tears after. And they may make no sense. They may be contradictory—first for this, then for just the opposite. They may not be logical, but they will be real.

Even after the initial shock has passed, you will be disturbed. For all your outward appearance, you will be anything but calm and stable. There may be times when you sit at a desk, stand at a stove, ride on a bus, and literally shake all over. You may lose part of your hearing or even faint periodically—with no past history or no physical cause. Or perhaps hysteria may become an old friend.

You may develop headaches, or stomachaches, or trembling hands, or loss of memory. You may become overactive for a period and then listless for another. You may fumble along or sit mindlessly daydreaming. You can think of nothing. You can react to nothing.

   Nothing comes
   and settles

                    and sits
                    and sits
                her bags are packed
                with mere nil
                    so heavy
                    so dead
                in every room
                she is sitting
                    just sitting ...

You may begin eating too much—you may have no appetite for food. You may have insomnia night after night—you may seek sleep as an escape.

            Sink
                into sleep
            The wonderful escape

            Head drooping
            Mind numbing, gratefully
            SLEEP!
                    Great Sleep
            I welcome you

            Be mine for now
            You're all I have.

You are bewildered; you cannot keep from musing again and again regarding the cause of your condition. Your reflections are exasperating, and you try unsuccessfully to stabilize your reactions. You look for logical explanations, for rationalizations, for ego-protective arguments, for answers ...

You wish you had professional help; you definitely do not want professional help. You desire to talk to someone and bare your soul; you refuse to talk to anyone and bare your soul. You yearn for the intelligence and insight to comprehend and act; you crave the simplicity and insensitivity to be unaware and passive.

And sometimes you digress—

When I was young,
a toddler still,
I had a dream
beyond my will.

And in the darkness
to my dread,
I saw a porcupine
beside my bed.

Night after night
he was there—
my dreadful symbol,
my thing of fear.

I miss that porcupine
beside my bed,
his quills seem harmless,
peaceful his head.

The beast is replaced
by pressure and strife,
the conflicts and pain,
the frustrations of life.

Instead of this horror,
oh, that I could will,
beside me now
a porcupine still!

You drift off to sleep, childhood prayers on your lips. . . .

Commit thy way unto the Lord;
Trust also in Him,
And He shall bring it to pass.
Psalm 37:5 KJV

Chapter 4

Pastor's Help

Blessed is he
whose transgressions are forgiven,
whose sins are covered.
Blessed is the man whose sin
the Lord does not count against him
and in whose spirit
is no deceit.
Psalm 32:1–2

For years you've attended church and seen your pastor at work. He's baptized, communed, preached, taught, confirmed, buried, and who knows what else. You've liked him very much for this, a little for that, and perhaps not at all for something else. You think you know your pastor fairly well ... perhaps you do. But you will get to know him better—much better.

For probably the first time in your life, you are desperately in need of a counselor. Spiritual, emotional, practical counseling—this is what you must have! You look around and see who's available, who could possibly help. No matter what assistance is forthcoming from family and friends, there is a special need that can only be filled by a pastor.

You feel that, for you, not just any minister will do. You'll need to expose your soul, your very being. You'll need to scrutinize your life, your feelings, your actions. You'll need to confess your sins. You'll need to hear God's forgiveness. You'll need to be assured of it. . . .

And so you want a minister who will be exceptionally loving and understanding—one who you feel will not be shocked or sit in judgment. Hopefully, you can turn to your

27

very own pastor. Now you will really get to know him—and he, you. If told in time, he will help you try to save your marriage; if not, he will help you adjust to its failure. He will let you talk and will talk to you, more frankly than you've ever experienced. He will advise you, encourage you, pray with and for you, and in such ways "love" you in witness of God's love.

But remember, he also will fail you. There will be times when he won't have the time or the ability or the patience to cope with one or another of your problems. He has no divine nature as our Lord—only a human nature. For all his love, your difficulties will not be the only ones in his concern. He will fail you—count on it! You can no more expect perfection of him than you do of yourself or anyone else.

Be grateful instead for all he does give you! He is evidence of the Spirit of God. Accept what he gives. You will remember his contribution for the remainder of your life. You will remember him as the personification of God's love.

Some ministers are
BLOOD AND THUNDER.
Flamboyantly fuming
the flambeau
of ferocity,
they assert God
at the expense of man.

Some ministers are
MASSIVE MILLSTONES
looping the letter of the Law,
until their aphorisms
asphyxiate.

But my minister
is just a man . . .
when he mounts
the pedestal
to preach,

he is still
on the
ground.
And when he holds out
his hand to heal,
this mere man
comforts.

Just a man . . .
who will pray
in your pathological
pit
and
descend
into your
depths
of dearth.
Embracing your pain,
searing your scar,
he is a handbook
to hope.

Just a man . . .
innately intense
and wise to the world,
he "sees" sin
in quadriphonic sound,
and with sagacious simplicity
grasps the Gospel
and lives
Love

The steadfast love of the Lord
is from everlasting to everlasting.
    Psalm 103:17 RSV

Chapter 5

Telling the News

Lord, I call to You;
*   come quickly to me.*
Hear my voice
*   when I call to You.*
May my prayer be set
*   before You like incense;*
may the lifting up of my hands
*   be like the evening sacrifice.*
                            Psalm 141:1–2

Only your very best friends know of your separation . . . and
you didn't tell them until you had to. . . . The neighbors have
started to wonder where your mate is; it won't be long before
everyone suspects. Yesterday you received a wedding invitation addressed to "Mr. and Mrs." It is bad enough to be
reminded of weddings—how are you going to gather the
courage to respond to an invitation for the two of you?

You keep answering phone calls for your husband. How
long will you be able to think up excuses for the absence?
And what do you say to old acquaintances who unknowingly
ask about your husband? There's no proper or satisfying way
to tell the truth. If you try to be light and casual, you may
appear callous and unfeeling. If you reveal inner fears and
frustrations, you may appear unbalanced or bitter.

Your friends are in the same awkward position. How do
they respond to the news? There is no "right way" for them
either. If they have run into your husband, should they tell
you or should they feign ignorance? In what way should they
become involved? Should they take sides? Can they become
involved without taking sides? They are unsure. They do not

know how to behave. They do not know what is expected of them from you ... from your spouse....

But their uncertainty is nothing compared to yours. You dread confrontations with people. You even dread attending church. You desperately need the assurance of God's love, but you desperately need to escape the questioning words or looks of members. You're sure some couples feel superior to you because they have stayed together for the better and the worse. You would just as soon avoid them. You know others will show only love, acceptance, and sympathy; but you'd just as soon avoid them too for now. Even sympathy can hurt—it points up your need so vividly.

You realize you'll have to take hold of yourself and start some plan of action. For one thing, you must admit that you're separated. You begin, for example, to start signing greeting cards with only your name, and sometimes you pen a brief note of explanation. You encourage those who know of the divorce to tell others so you can avoid embarrassment.

You begin correcting yourself when you refer to "we" instead of "I" in conversations. This is not easy, for years of habit do not soon reverse, and it's difficult to rephrase what is natural. You are not widowed, however, and references to the ex-mate will more likely evoke curiosity or disapproval than matter-of-factness or understanding. So you try ... you try to change your speech. Yet day after day you find yourself slipping into the old patterns.

Faith in your marriage gone, your attitude towards other people's is also changing. You are slightly envious over what they have, but also slightly suspect. You wonder if, put to the test, their marriages would endure.

> Simple—
>   unlittered—
>   unhampered—
>   unreal.
> Happiness with icing ...
>   don't ask for cake,
>   it may exist.

You start noticing flaws in friends' marriages. Now and then the partners point them out to you; perhaps they think the admission will be comforting. Some muse how lucky you are; oh, if they had their independence! They complain about this or that lack in their mates and even look to you for sympathy. They confide in you, yet they don't know quite how to take you now that you are "available." You are to be pitied . . . on the other hand, you could develop into a threat.

You reflect on your own marriage disaster. You reflect on the sandpits in others' marriages. You begin to think of the world of the married as the world of the superficial—a mere facade of happiness. You've taken off your wedding band, and it's as if you stepped outside and are looking into the window of a dated institution.

You begin to doubt if you could ever love again. The married around you don't seem truly happy; maybe there is no such state. Perhaps you have been desiring the wrong thing. Perhaps the only way to achieve peace and happiness is to let nothing get through to you . . . to let nothing move you.

> I have observed the statues,
> Self-composed and silent . . .
> And I envy their fixed smiles.
> I am jealous of their hard strength
> And their unbending essence.
> The statues are lasting,
> Their emotion unchanged.
> They are calm, content, and cold. . . .
>
> Someday I will be as you,
>   marble throughout . . .
> And they will look
>   and pass on . . . .
> And though one pauses to touch,
>   *I* will be untouched.
> Though they move me about,
>   *I* will remain unmoved.

And if they melt me and recast,
    I will mold the mold.
Strong as steel,
    hard as diamond,
        fixed as eternity.
I will observe these *plastics* with *pity.*

You are a doubter.

You know God loves . . .

But few are like God . . . .

Create in me a clean heart, O God,
    and renew a right spirit within me.
Cast me not away from Thy presence,
    and take not Thy Holy Spirit from me.
Restore unto me the joy of Thy salvation,
    and uphold me with Thy free Spirit.
    Psalm 51:10–12 KJV

Chapter 6

Family Help

Hasten, O God, to save me;
O Lord, come quickly to help me. . . .
I am poor and needy;
come quickly to me, O God.
You are my help and my deliverer;
O Lord, do not delay.
Psalm 70:1, 5

For all the times you wanted independence from your parents or siblings in the past, you need them now. If they live nearby, you consult with them often. You tell them your problems so often they know the words by memory. And even if they don't really know how to help, they try; and that's all you ask. You appreciate them as you never have before.

> You, my sister
>   lately appreciated
>   dearly, dearly loved
> Because you are you
>   I am blessed.

If your family lives elsewhere, you beg them to come and stay for a time. Phone calls, letters, short visits all help, but you meet each new day with fear you won't make it through. In the darkest of night you call out for your mother, just as you did when you needed her as a child. And you are comforted, just remembering . . . .

> Mother
>
> In all the world
> the one who feels
>   exactly . . .

Especially in sorrow,
> and in need of solace,
I call to you . . .
you
> my mother

In times as this
> you come to me.
In times as this
> no one is closer.
Lightly
> I feel your touch of love.
Softly
> I hear your words of comfort
Completely
> I experience you.
You . . .
> all that is you . . .
and for that moment
> I need no more . . .

Mother

In all the world
the one who feels
> exactly . . .

Depressed and discouraged, you may not be able to camouflage your condition from your children. Once in a while even your youngest may literally embrace and comfort you when you lose emotional control. Then again, just recalling the strength and loving spirit of a Christian parent will abate your loneliness. You'll feel refreshed and vow to allow nothing to ever take that gift away from you.

Unless you are a statistical exception, your ex-husband's family seems to have forgotten you. You mourn the loss of those you loved. You yearn for their understanding . . . even when it's not possible.

During the long days and nights you cannot forget your

divorce. You are so lonely. You are so separated. You are so cut off. . . .

> I am so lonely tonight—
> so alone—
> walking aimlessly,
> wanting to talk, to share, to love . . . .
>
> The baby cries into the night
> asking for consolation—easy to give.
>
> Nothing consoles me,
> no tranquillizer eases the lifeless
> numbing of the spine,
> the sick deadness within . . .
> Nothing dulls the active mind.
>
> Oh, for a friend now,
> someone to listen to laugh,
> to comfort—to cry!
> I stand by empty
> "until death do us part"
>
> I am so lonely tonight—
> so alone—

Whatever loneliness means to the child or the single person, it means something quite different to you. Your marriage has been torn apart. You remember it as a whole union; now it is an amputee. There exists a loneliness of incompleteness that only the formerly married realize. You tell God about it night after night. You figure He knows what it's like, but you tell Him anyway, just to make sure. You cast your care upon Him, for you know He cares for you.

> *I lift up my eyes to You,*
> *to You whose throne is*
> *in the heavens.*
> *Psalm 123:1*

Chapter 7

Children

Lo, children are a heritage of the Lord;
and the fruit of the womb is His reward.

Our sons in their youth
will be like well-nurtured plants,
and our daughters will be like pillars
carved to adorn a palace.
Psalm 144:12

When the marriage chain first broke, your children seemed doomed. Surely this would destroy them! At the very least, they'd never lead normal lives. You could forget about carefree, happy childhood days for them. Theirs would be most unhappy and maladjusted.

The fears were intense and genuine. And in a way, your spouse shared them but was unable to compensate. You were frantic and appreciated any offer of help, even if it might fail. Things were desperate in those nothing-made-sense days. Humpty Dumpty had fallen off the wall, and nothing could put him back together again.

If your children were not with you, you missed them terribly. You didn't know which was worse—not seeing them, or visiting them and then missing them all the more later. You were on a treadmill, and the ache was constant.

If you did have your children, they may have been the one thing that kept you going through the darkest days. No matter what their age, toddler or teen-ager, they needed you. You would have to be their rock of love. You may not have been capable of it yet. You may still have been in that numb stage. But if they and you were to make it, you would have to make it together ... somehow.

> Live
> In a perambulator
> And you never need walk ...

You were frightened. Raising children was difficult enough within marriage—you didn't want the responsibility alone. You felt you couldn't cope with it, at least surely not at this time.

Even if time changed your reactions and fears regarding the children, some of the same concerns remain. If you have custody of the children, you're conscious of their many needs. There are the obvious physical ones, of course—food, clothing, shelter. These never posed the problem during your marriage that they do now. No matter how poor you were in the past, you are worse off now. Money—where will enough come from?

You must find a job. Or you must find a better job. There simply isn't enough money to pay the bills. While people can talk about child support being such a help, you know it will barely cover child care while you work. And if where you work has no child care center, whom will you find to watch the children during the day? Who will give them the special love and care they need so badly now? Whom can you trust? After a hard day at work, how will you be both the good father and mother to them? You simply don't know. But things will get better, you think—they will have to!

Now and then, just when everything seems on an even keel, a crisis arises. A child gets very ill, or falls off a porch, or swallows adult medication. You may need to rush the child to the hospital, but you have no way to get there. You look frantically for someone to take you, and you also need someone to baby-sit. When you eventually get to a doctor, you'll worry how you will pay the fee. And when you buy the prescriptions, you'll wonder how you'll balance the food budget later. But now your child is sick; that's all that matters! You feel ill, too, but so differently. ...

My little son
is
sick.
And so
he
sleeps.
How healthy
his
        illness
            is . . .

Much of your energy directed towards your children's needs goes towards their emotional and spiritual ones. They need to be loved—to be totally and completely immersed in love! God loves them—they must always be assured of that. And your love, no matter how great, will have to grow.

Children want their parents together; they want whole families, not fragmented ones. They'll do anything for this end. They may cry, beg, scold, reprimand, or even use logic. And when nothing works, they want to know why . . . they want to know the truth. You will not be able to hedge off their questions forever, and it is better to be honest from the beginning. To deceive the children now will only hurt them more later. You'll level with them . . . and then level them with love.

But what explanations will help ease their loss? What rationalizations will compensate? Their questions may go on for years. Perhaps they'll never really understand—you sometimes wonder if you do yourself, completely. . . . Fathers who desire divorce face the accusations of their children. Mothers who grant divorce may also be accused. It is a terrifying thought. You've lost enough love; you don't want to lose your children's also.

Have you ever killed something,
        knowing it would not die?
But somewhere, in a life apart

it lives—and yet is dead.
And your children will ask you
   why you did it.
What will you answer? The truth?
   That it wanted to die ...
Will they believe you?

And the dead will live,
   separated ...
And the living will live,
   separated ...
Never completely understanding
   the madness, the mess,
Young and idealistic,
Condemning the cheating,
You will not fulfill their lack
Any more than they will understand your act.

Teach them to swim
Let no cramps strangle their emotions,
Make them stronger
And then pray
They never need the strength,
That, somehow, beyond all logic,
They know as you,
That love existed in your loveless act.

Your children will be torn between love for you and love for their father. Their allegiance will be divided and may stay that way. You cannot expect anything different.

Your ex-husband and you have failed your children, and you will never make it up to them. Yet you must do everything you can to prove to your children that you are constant, to prove that you will not leave them, to prove that you will love them always.

You continue your day-by-day effort to show your affection. You know that material means will not assure it. What material proofs will comfort a child who cries through a nightmare or sits starry-eyed in a trance? What material proofs would ever compensate for a lost father?

No, there are other, more effective ways to show love. You can take more time to pray and play with your youngsters. You can hold the little ones on your lap; you can rock them; you can read and sing to them. You can sit by the older ones as they watch TV, and you can put your arm around them or hold their hand as you talk together. You can pray together and discuss your faith and the constancy of our Lord, who never leaves us and who never reneges on His love. You can worship together and make it an occasion of joy. You can share all types of indoor and outdoor activities with your children. And you can say, "I love you. I'm proud of you. I'm grateful God has given you to me."

The message should be repeated, one way or another, again and again. As you heal your children, you will be healed. They will help you through difficult hours. It is a two-way street, this street of love.

> Today you smiled
>   and your laughter
>   caught my heart.
> Today you smiled
>   and it was enough
> If today you smile
>   tomorrow will I?

The peaceful, joyous side of your nature that you present to your children may be more a brave front than reality. You still need help. *You* still need to be comforted.

And all through the weeks and months you're working to help "heal" your children, you wonder what is going through the mind of the ex-husband. You wonder if the children are remembered in that special way only a parent knows . . . .

> Do you hear
>   the cry in the night?

When all is still,
and the world in slumber,
are you awakened by the cry ...
the personal, needful cry of your own?
Does it reach past the miles
of city lights and night traffic
to where you lie, alone?

Do you see as I, or
does the darkness protect you?
    blotting out images?
Can a future cheer you,
    fulfilling all desires?
Or will you always know?
Will you always love?
Will you always respond?

Do you think
you will always hear
    the cry in the night?

That special cry,
    just for you ...

You don't know the answer. But *your* special cry is heard.
You've cried it often enough to God. Surely He's heard it ...
hasn't He? When will He answer?
    When?

> *How long, O Lord?*
>   *Will you forget me forever?*
> *How long will You hide Your face from me?*
>   *Psalm 13:1*

Chapter 8

Means of Coping

O Lord, You have seen this;
*   be not silent.*
Do not be far from me, O Lord.
    Psalm 35:22

"How are you getting along?" your doctor asks. "Just barely," you say. "Haven't you got something that will help my temperament?"

You're over the hysteria and other extreme forms of physical reactions now, but you still lack the stability of your predivorce days. The period of depression has been replaced by a nervous, fidgety one. You try to control it most of the time, but whenever the condition is combined with weariness, problems, or setbacks of any kind, you find yourself snapping or even yelling at anyone nearby.

> Someone
> took a rubber band,
> knotted it in my
> cranium
> and then began to
> twist . . .
>
> Beautifully
> unfolding
> in a blooming
> blossom,
> radiating the back
> with taut
> torture
>
> Someone

had unmitigated nerve
to take my nerve
of crystal china
and
chisel
and
chip

Stand BACK!

When I SCREAM,
the shrill
will
shatter,
the rubber band
will
reverberate,
the lymphs
will
limp.

You desperately yearn to relax. You're tired of the back-ache, headache, stomachache, or any other physical ache that characterizes the condition. You're tired of insomnia, yet this "tiredness" doesn't help put you to sleep.

Over the months you try or consider all the world's stan-dard remedies. If you overate before, you double your habit. The appeal of drinking to a "nonfeeling stage" may be great enough to overcome even an aversion for alcohol. Perhaps drugs have become a temptation—at least the kind doctors can prescribe. You're tempted to try all sorts of means you'd never consider in better days, and you pray for the strength to withstand such urges. You know that:

No temptation has siezed you except what is common to man. And God is faithful; He will not let you be tempted beyond what you can bear. But when you are tempted, He will also provide a way out so that you can stand up under it.

1 Corinthians 10:13

You reflect on God's words and comfort. Like King Saul, you may let music—spiritual music—calm you during difficult periods. You worship, sing, pray, and read your Scriptures, but there are times when you almost think it's all a sham. Doubt flickers here and there, and you pray for more evidence of our Lord's reality and His love.

The Holy Spirit answers and strengthens you in many ways—one, through His people. God uses people to help people. He uses your pastor, your family, and your friends to help you ... just as He will someday use you to help others.

There *are* Christians who take seriously our Lord's words:

> As the Father has loved Me, so have I loved you. Now remain in My love .... Love each other as I have loved you.
>
> *John 15:9, 12*

Or those of St. John:

> Let us love one another, for love comes from God. Everyone who loves has been born of God and knows God.
>
> *1 John 4:7*

The Spirit will provide at least one person who will be a friend—who will show you the Father's love through his or her love. This friend may not understand exactly what you're going through, but will *try* to understand and will be as close to empathizing as any "outsider" can be. And you will value the friend greatly.

> It is a rare experience
> when one enjoys the unique friendship

that is ours ...
A rapport that neither can explain,
as we cannot say
we always agree,
nor do we always perceive
the reality of each other's world.
Yet there is a depth
in each
the other cannot deny,
and there is an honesty
few would unmask.

I surely thank God
for this bond that lives
within the void
of both distance and time.
For if we saw the other not
and lived a hundred years before again we met,
we would be friends
close still
because of that unique reality
that defies description,
that unexplainable existence
that escapes the mind's grasp,
that living appreciation
that I know
you know.
Of individual dancing
to a high frequency
we can both
hear.

Although all in the body of Christ with whom you worship
Sunday after Sunday cannot be the one unique friend just
mentioned, they can be a comfort just by their existence.
Coming together to commune with God and His people can
be the greatest joy you'll ever know. As you participate in

Communion, this joyous feast at the altar of God, you'll be assured that you have been forgiven, that you are loved, and that you will be strengthened. With the angels and archangels and, yes, all the company of saints in heaven and on earth, you will be praising God in peace and joy.

Praise the Lord.
Praise God in His sanctuary;
praise Him in His mighty heavens.
Praise Him for His acts of power;
praise Him for His surpassing greatness.
Praise Him with the sounding of the trumpet,
praise Him with the harp and lyre,
praise Him with tambourine and dancing,
praise Him with the strings and flute,
praise Him with the clash of cymbals,
praise Him with resounding cymbals.
Let everything that has breath
praise the Lord.
Praise the Lord.
Psalm 150

Chapter 9

Ex-Mate

Then our mouth was filled with laughter,
and our tongue with songs of joy.
Psalm 126:2 RSV

There is a bit of the romantic in everybody. We tend to think
that life should have storybook endings. We begin our marriages with the assumption that marital problems will be min-
imal and we will live happily ever after. And even when we
have been separated or divorced against our wishes, we believe that someday the nightmare will be over and the old
love will bloom again.

If we were the party who wanted the divorce, it may have
been because we thought we weren't appreciated. "He didn't
understand me" is so common a complaint it has become a
cliché. And if we didn't want the divorce, we felt our husband
certainly didn't appreciate us. If he had only appreciated our
love, we feel, things would have turned out differently. We
really don't understand our ex-partner. How is it he missed
this most obvious love of ours?

> I look at you
> and wonder
> why ...
>
> I once knew you.
> I'm sure I
> did ...
> You were what I
> wasn't
> And I knew
> myself ...

But now
who are you
anyway?
I was found
in loving
you,
While you were
lost
with love ...

Time is odd ...
You can
give me explanations
tomorrow,
But make me happy
yesterday ...

Yet because we did not succeed in marriage, our egos are crushed, our self-esteem is low. In the back of our mind is the suspicion—yes, fear—that we may not have what it takes to remain married. We want to eventually prove ourselves in a new union, yet we dread the test—what if we should fail again? We're no longer sure of ourselves or who we are.

Why analyze?
ACT!
Though never a
gambler,
You dare not
avoid
fear.
If once
and for all
is possible,
Jump!

FALL!
even,

But know
WHO
Is falling,
So that mirrors
Mean
something.

Meanwhile in this new setting is the presence of our former marriage—just behind us, yet still here. Though it is dissolved, some ties remain. For one reason or another, we may come in contact with our ex-husband. And in discussing the visiting of the children, or the selling of the house, or the dividing of the joint property, or whatever, we find ourselves in an almost-married/almost-not-married situation.

We were divorced, amiably or angrily, yet there is still a "marriage memory" which only time can erase. There is even an attraction on occasion, and the meetings we have may very well develop into courting experiences, both consciously and unconsciously. Each partner may act more considerately to the other than they have in years. They may dress especially nice, for example, or prepare an excellent meal, or listen intently to a story they've heard dozens of times previously, forgetting for an interim all that passed between them in the near past.

The habit of a marriage—the years of living together—is very strong. But sooner or later, and usually sooner, the bubble bursts. Natural, negative characteristics of the partners, so irksome to each other, arise within a conversation or even within a somewhat romantic interlude. The rose-colored glasses break—the prince turns back into a frog, and Cinderella back into a scouring maid.

We feel very much like the guinea pigs and rats used in learning experiments—rats that are conditioned to pull levers for a reward. The day comes when the rewards cease, but the rats go on pulling the same levers anyway . . . to no avail. We wonder when we will finally learn that the ex-mate is no longer the answer for us. We know we learn most everything by experience. It seems *this* lesson will have to be learned more than once.

> Little rat
> In the box
> How often
> Will you
> Pull?

> How often
> Will they polish
> The familiar lever
> To make it
> Glow
> Promisingly ...

> Little rat,
> Pensive and
> Still,
> The lever looks
> Gold,
> Your paws turn
> Green

> If learning is
> Learned
> How long?
> How
> Long?

There seems to be no stronger relationship than that of husband and wife, and the memories of a past union will never be completely erased. But although we will never be able to completely eradicate the experience because of its unique-ness, so also we will never again look at it for our help, for our comfort, for our life ... no, not today ... no, not in the many tomorrows to come. ...

Now, however, we feel alone. We have nothing human

to fill the empty place in our heart. And so we turn to our Creator for help.

> I lift up my eyes to the hills—
>> where does my help come from?
> My help comes from the Lord,
>> the Maker of heaven and earth.
>>> *Psalm 121:1–2*

It is God who will be a Refuge and our Strength. It is God who will sustain us. It may not seem that way now. It may seem little is sustaining us. The God of Abraham and Deborah . . . the God of Paul and Priscilla . . . our God . . . may seem a far way off. But hold on!

> *Wait on the Lord:*
> *be of good courage,*
> *and He shall strengthen*
> *thy heart.*
> *Wait,*
> *I say,*
> *on the Lord.*
>> *Psalm 27:14 KJV*

Chapter 10

Dating

In You, O Lord, I have taken refuge;
let me never be put to shame.
Psalm 71:1

People look at you strangely nowadays. You don't feel any different, but others seem to think you are. Even your new title has discriminatory connotations. You are labeled a *divorcée,* and everyone knows and apparently believes the cliché about divorcées. The conditions of your divorce make no difference; you are stuck with the degrading tag. Whatever your married moral scruples were, it is presumed you now have lost them, and sooner or later someone will drop a hint to that effect. Perhaps you'll even experience that unpleasant overture—the proposition of a married man who's the husband of a friend. There are always some who assume that all a divorcee needs is sexual satisfaction to make all her problems disappear. And it is always this same "brilliant" type who is "noble" enough to offer his services.

As for you, you want and need to begin a whole new social life. You turn to the church but may find you have no niche. Highest esteem is given to the married state (notwithstanding St. Paul's opinion), and many a couple feels you should date for one purpose only—to remarry. Nothing short of remarriage is honorable, whether you are ready for it or not.

You may have members in your congregation who introduce you to fellow Christians you find interesting. But if this does not happen, you will probably look elsewhere. You need companionship other than that of your unhappy memories, and you may turn to the secular world to find it. The reaction towards divorce there ranges from hostility to ambivalence. Yet on the surface most people project a "live and let live" attitude. People you meet are just "getting by" in life themselves. They have their own problems. They have no faith . . . they have no solutions . . . they cannot "help" you.

The church did not speak to your needs, seemingly, and neither do those newfound friends and acquaintances. But at first you may be very happy with their matter-of-factness towards your divorce. It is nice to be accepted as normal rather than as somewhat abnormal. And it's reassuring to find other people with insecurity problems. You had thought you were alone in this respect.

At secular gatherings you notice more and more of life's emotional cripples—insecure people who so obviously need to blow their own horn that they make spectacles of themselves. You may even meet one whose ridiculous claims range from winning a war singlehandedly to mastering a language that doesn't exist.

> He really impressed me
> (course I'm easily impressed . . .)

> He had traveled the world
> And had mastered its speech.
> In France he spoke French,
> In Russia, of course Russian,
> Germany, German,
> Spain, Spanish,
> et cetera, et cetera . . .
> This exceptional linguist,
> This great man of letters,
> This worldwide traveler.

> But what made him unique,
> What impressed me no end,
> Was the boast: "In Egypt
> I spoke Egyptian!"

> Impressed without,

Laughing within,
"Amazing!" said I
As I watched him die. . . .

(But then I'm easily impressed,
Impressed easily am I . . . .)

Once you've entered these new circles, it isn't long before
you begin to find people who are just like you—who are also
divorced. You notice it seems more relaxing to talk to them
than to most other people. An immediate rapport is common
when two divorced people are introduced and left to con-
verse. You find you can make a remark about your situation
or past marriage and the other will respond with "I know
exactly!" Once divorced, a person does know exactly . . .
exactly.

And so the divorced form a new element—a world unto
themselves. Once introduced, it will amaze you that outsiders
are so unaware of it. This unique new world functions within
the framework of the larger one, yet its members recognize
each other and indicate the recognition right under the noses
of the nonmembers. Indeed, as you meet more and more
people in this new setting, you may begin to think of divorced
friends and acquaintances as insiders, and of married, widowed, and other single people as outsiders.

The pull towards others like you can be very strong. It
can be so strong, in fact, that you must recognize that it could
pull you away from others like you in Christ—from the family
of God. For it is this family, after all, that is the healthiest for
you. It is within this family that you will experience the greatest comfort, peace, healing, and joy. It is the Spirit who guides
and sustains you each day of your life. And unless He also
governs the lives of your new friends, they will bring you no
lasting happiness.

You will also meet widowers among your new contacts.
Nevertheless, although they also are without mates, you will
have little in common with them and may find them less than
satisfactory dates. Their allegiances are to the dead, while you

have no such loyalty to your former spouse. And their memories of their marriages may be strong barriers to any new relationships you hope to build. You need to find yourself and to improve your self-esteem. You do not need someone who looks upon his or her married life as a success and upon yours as a failure.

But you *do* want to begin dating, and three out of four people do so within a year of their divorce. What you don't realize is that it's a whole new ball game out there. If you last dated back in the days when the big question was whether or not a kiss was appropriate for a first date, you're in for an eye-opener. No matter how sophisticated you think you may be, you aren't.

Dating is a game, and everybody's got their own set of rules. What is shocking or startling to the newly divorced Christian is the rules that are accepted as standard among formerly married men and women. A sexual pass is not uncommon for first dates, and often it is an obvious and somewhat crude pass.

Females who are new to such passes usually consider their dates's proposal degrading. They may react to the "insult" with fear, or then again, with great rage. And they're especially insulted when asked if they have a sexually transmitted disease!

Your biggest decision in any male-female relationship you enter is to clarify who you are, what your needs are, and how best you can fulfill your needs without compromising your nature as a child of God. This is a decision, perhaps a struggle, you must make with yourself and with your Lord. But it is one you cannot put off . . . because the rest of the world is not going to change.

Your happily married friends may be the first to give you advice and the last to understand your needs—theirs, after all, are taken care of. Some might even be shocked if you tried to explain that your divorce did not neutralize your gender. But *you* know it hasn't. And you know you are insecure. And you know you need love and acceptance. And you know you are subject to temptation. And you know better than to expect change in the "system."

> For a while
>> I thought this one was different ...
> I who have learned
>> they are all the same.
> I who suspect
>> we are all the same ...
> Imagine ...
>> Just imagine ...
> If I won, obviously
>> he lost.
> All right, so I won.
>> Did I?
> Why can't I stay
>> with one conclusion?
> Why do I sigh with relief
>> and still want to kick myself?
> Why can't I always trust myself?
> More important,
>> Why don't I always want to?

> Bless you Naiveté!
> Bless you Righteous Conscience!
> Bless you Contentment!
> Bless you Stupidity!
> Damn the Makers of 100 Assorted Flavors!
> Damn the Market Appeal!
> Damn the Distracting Distributors!
> Damn the Curious Taste Buds!
> Double Damn the Starving System!

> Prepare to wrestle
>> with the Angel of the Lord.
> You will write the end
>> of this chapter
> afterwards ....

The Lord is near to all
*   who call on Him,*
to all who call on Him in truth.
He fulfills the desires of those
*   who fear Him;*
He hears their cry
*   and saves them.*
The Lord watches over all
*   who love Him.*
*   Psalm 145:18–20*

Chapter 11

Extreme Doubt, Faith Challenged

I cried out to God . . . .
My soul refused to be comforted.
I remembered You, O God, and I groaned;
I mused, and my spirit grew faint . . .
I was too troubled to speak . . .
Will the Lord reject forever?
Will He never show His favor again?
Has His unfailing love vanished forever?
Has His promise failed for all time?
Has God forgotten to be merciful?
Has He in anger withheld His compassion?
Psalm 77:1–4, 7–9

Has God indeed forgotten you? Has He forgotten Himself? Who is He, anyway? And who are you?

Somewhere along the line you seem to have lost your identity. Now you're not really sure who you are. One personality is a ghostly shadow of the old you; one is a parent role; one is a professional image; one a social spirit; and so on. What it all adds up to is 1 and 1 and 1 and . . . and . . . but never a sum total. You've changed, you know, but you don't know *who* you've changed into . . . .

> What am I thinking about?
> I don't know, really
> I just think . . .
> Everything runs together,
> And yet there's no pattern.
> Not happy, not bitter,

I feel like an old woman
Recalling memories,
Some warm, some sad,
Yet even the sadness is warm,
A poignant warmth,
A part of life.
It's as if I have
Something to say,
Something to tell,
And yet I can't tell
Without destroying.
And anyway, you'd nod
But not know ...

One begins to breathe
When oxygen is removed.
After the initial gasping,
Choking and dying,
You lie so still
While life seeps slowly back
Through each little pore.
And though you
Again use a windpipe,
It is never enough.
Some cell here
Breathes one way,
Another far off
Wants something else.
Every tiny cell,
Small in itself,
Yet a distraction
With memories,
A demand
Of emotions.
Each cell conflicting
Yet each a part of you.

There is no quick grief period for divorce. The same reactions, in varying degrees, occur again and again in the months (and sometimes years) that follow. There is pain, and dying, and flashes of freedom, and then again disappointment. There is experimenting in new life styles, and then depression when they fail to live up to hopes. There is dormancy and apathy—colorless periods which cloud your vision of God, yourself, and even a relationship between you that is normally whole and vital.

I don't know, God
You seem so far ...
It's me, I'm
Sure
But somehow
You don't seem
Real

Are You only here
When I need You?
Even I know
Better

I've been existing so long
Without You
Really
Oh, I talk of You
But not really
to You

I think my soul is dressed
In gray
No, not even gray
Just sort of
Nothing ...
Somewhere it lost
Its brightly colored
Frock

When You find it
Will You bring it back

To me?

I think if I had it
I'd see You again
I think if I had it
I'd know where
I am

Perhaps your uncertainty and self-doubts stem from the old questions which have never been answered: Why? What failed? Was it I? Should I have? Should I have not? What good will come from it? Why did it happen?

During the darker hours of periods like this you have no idea that the future holds brighter days. They can be right around the corner, but they may as well be a planet away. You cannot see the dim dusk of tomorrow, let alone the bright sunshine of a month or year away. You know only suspicion, and doubt, and uncertainty, and a fear of new beginnings. God has humbled you. There are periods of introspection which leave you stripped of any dignity and of all merit. You've recognized the innermost parts of your being and have confessed with Paul, "I am the foremost of sinners" (1 Timothy 1:15 RSV).

You have been wounded; you have been bitter; you have been in pain; but you have never yet cursed your Maker. Always you have clung to the reality of God's love; even when you wanted to escape it, it followed you as the "hound of heaven." You could not shake off your faith. You could not run from your God. No, if you fled to the heavens, He was at the top; if you peered into chasms, He was at the bottom. However dim your flame of faith, you could not snuff it out. You clung to that tiny match barely glowing in the blizzard around you. It was the eye of the tornado—the source of perfect peace. Even when you didn't realize it, it was the staple that stapled you.

If anyone were to have told you that you'd ever give up on God, you would have responded as Peter did—perhaps others, but never you. Still, you have doubts that mount daily;

there are, in fact, times when you reflect on your naiveté in ever believing that belief itself would be a cure-all, or that the Scriptures could be words of comfort rather than meaningless syllables not backed by love in evidence. Nevertheless, to give up on God? To deny His validity? To question His promise?

Yet it's possible. You may do all this ... and more.... If you are disappointed once too often, if you have one too many straws placed on your back, if you wear out before rest refreshes—well, then, you may just lose your Job patience. You may have "had it" with life. You may spill out pent-up emotions in an uncontrolled attack on God Himself. You may begin a prayer, turn it into a curse, and end it in defeat. You will be shocked by your audacity. But like a dam burst, nothing will stop you until the winds of the hurricane have exhausted themselves.

> Dear God,
>   Help Me!
> You're the only one who cares ...
> The only one who's true ...
> The only one I can trust ...
>
> What a fool I was,
> What a fool I am!
> Day by day I see
> How weak, how naive
>   I am.
> How much humbling do I need?
> God help me!
>
> God, don't try me anymore.
> I am prostrate.
> I give in.
> I can't bear more.
> If we are playing a game,
> I concede.
> End it.
> I can't go on.

God, I who need forgiveness
Can't forgive You.

Have You no pity?
No love at all?
Do You laugh too?
Are You the devil disguised?
Forgive me, but
I am sick of Your trials,
Sick to death of Your tests.
I never pass, anyway.
Just leave me alone!

Don't You Dare
    use me as Job . . .
Find another!
I refuse to be Your example!
If this is what You are,
If this is what You expect,
If this is what You demand,
I renounce You.
I am sorry I every heard of You!
I regret the day I turned to You
Because You refused to help!
    I must help myself.
    What need of You?

God, why?
Forgive me my failings.
I want to believe,
But even You
Have failed me.

You should be terrified at your words . . . but your faith
is not that awake. You have given up on God; you feel He has
deserted you like all the rest. You hope it will not last—this
doubt—but you do not know.

Right now it is too real to believe it will ever be otherwise.

Night pierces my bones,
>   my gnawing pains never rest.
In His great power God becomes
>   like clothing to me;
He binds me like the neck
>   of my garment.
He throws me into the mud,
>   and I am reduced to dust and ashes.
I cry out to You, O God, but You do not answer;
>   I stand up, but You merely look at me.
You turned on me ruthlessly;
>   with the might of Your hand
>   You attack me.
>   *Job 30:17–21*

Perhaps for the first time in your life you know what total desertion is . . . Perhaps for the first time in your life you know what hell must be . . . Perhaps for the first time in your life you understand the enigma of our Lord's cry from the cross:

>   Eloi, Eloi, lama sabachthani? . . .
>   My God, My God, why have You forsaken Me?
>   *Mark 15:34*

The Lord is silent. He does not speak. He does not hear. He must not care.

Perhaps for the first time in your life the Psalms *really* become yours . . . .

>   *My God, my God, why have You forsaken me?*
>   *Why are You so far from saving me,*
>   *so far from the words of my groaning?*
>   *O my God, I cry out by day*
>   *but You do not answer,*
>   *by night,*
>   *and am not silent.*
>   *Psalm 22:1–2*

Chapter 12

Recovery from Doubt, Faith Rebuilt

The fool says in his heart,
"There is no God."
Psalm 53:1

For an hour, a day, a month, perhaps years, you may doubt. You may believe that God, if there is a God, has cast you aside—has forgotten you. You may ignore Him completely or bewail your fate and cry as did Job:

> May the day of my birth perish . . . .
> Why did I not perish at birth,
>   and die as I came from the womb? . . .
> I have no peace, no quietness . . . .
> The night drags on,
>   and I toss till the dawn . . . .
> When He passes me, I cannot see Him;
>   when He goes by, I cannot see Him.
> *Job 3:3, 11, 26; 7:4; 9:11*

You don't believe. And "unless you see signs and wonders you will not believe" (John 4:48 RSV). The present is so overwhelmingly real, you cannot see into the future. But it's there. And God has a plan for you in it. "God is greater than man" (Job 33:12 RSV). And He can take the greatest evil that happens to you and bring good out of it. For "we know that in everything God works for good with those who love Him" (Romans 8:28 RSV).

There is a reason God chastens you . . . or allows you to be chastened. God gives you a new chance for a new life. He silently observes your moods of doubt and self-pity; He patiently listens to your endless complaints; but then He finally roars back, *"Just who do you think you are to question Me?"*

> Where were you
> > when I laid the earth's foundations? ...
> Does the hawk take flight by your wisdom
> > and spread his wings toward the south?
> Does the eagle soar at your command
> > and build his nest on high? ...
> Will the one who contends with the Almighty
> > correct Him?
> Let Him who accuses God answer Him!
> > *Job 38:4; 39:26–27; 40:2*

But you have no answers.... You still don't understand God, though you begin to believe enough to be frightened. Your faith starts to thaw out, and you marvel at your previous audacity. Yet, for all of your unfaithfulness, you hear the Almighty telling you to relax and put your trust in Him. He assures you that "all things are possible to him who believes" (Mark 9:23 RSV). Your answer is a cry, "[Lord], I believe; help my unbelief!" (Mark 9:24 RSV) You cling to the hope that God *has* control ... that God *does* care ... and that God *can* change your life....

> God does all these things to a man—
> > twice, even three times—
> to turn back his soul from the pit,
> > that the light of life may shine on him.
> > *Job 33:29*

You begin to realize that what happened to you was not God's will, for the God who is Love wills only good for His loved ones. You know that your quarrel is not with God, that you are contending not "against flesh and blood, but against the rulers, against the authorities, against the powers of this dark world and against the spiritual forces of evil in the heavenly realms" (Ephesians 6:12). And you say to God, "You can't let me fight this alone. I need more help. I need You!"

You remind God of His covenant with you. Luther said when we are oppressed by sin or conscience we must retort, "But I am baptized! And if I am baptized, I have the promise that I shall be saved, and have eternal life, both in soul and body!"

So you remind God of your Baptism and of His promise of love. You hold Him to it. You hang on even if He doesn't seem to notice you. You are one of His children; and even if you weren't, you could demand at least "the crumbs that fall from their master's table" (Matthew 15:27). You "wait for the Lord" (Psalm 27:14), but you don't give up. And He *does* come. If you ask Him, He does come . . . perhaps "in a dream, in a vision of the night" (Job 33:15), perhaps in a rush of the Spirit, perhaps in a quiet rebuilding of confidence and faith in Him. But He *will come* . . . because *He is* . . . .

In the name of the
Father
Son
and Holy Spirit
Amen

Dear Lord,
Dear Friend,

I've stopped walking
to think
And crying
to pray
And fighting
to submit

And You are right . . .

Jacob wrestled an angel.
Did I
unknowing?

I am exhausted
     weak
Raggedy Ann,
Straw strewn on the floor,

My head drops,
My senses sag,
And I would sleep
     would sleep
     would sleep
Through roaring scores
Of Catskill pins

Glorious Lord,
To give one
This composing point
When frame no longer
     can resist,
And mind, encased,
     must rest.

I thank You, God,
For strength that surrounds
And seeps within,
Till I would rise and shout
     "God's here!
     Right here!
     He stays
And sustains
And secures
     ME!"

As a rug whipped
I am dustless.
If anyone walks,
My fibers stand firm.

Just a short while ago you had a shaken faith . . . and no
hope. You were as good as dead.

My spirit is broken, my days are cut short,
the grave awaits me. . . .
Where then is my hope?
Job 17:1, 15

But now all has changed. Now the prayer of your loved
ones has been answered: "May the God of hope fill you with
all joy and peace as you trust in Him, so that you may overflow
with hope by the power of the Holy Spirit" (Romans 15:13).
Now you know:

There is a Holy Spirit!
As real as sodium chloride
on the cheek . . .
Yes, more so . . .
And there is sin,
Yes, and so personal
too personal . . .
too narcistic . . .
I have to get away
to see the mirror
And it's a shock—
the impatience
I see,
and the sin
of self-love
and will
But it's a joy—
God's love and peace
Because they erase the image,
and the Holy Spirit
gives hope
and help!
And tears of remorse
are as a
Baptism . . .

God has seen you through this . . . in spite of yourself. He will see you through the future . . . in spite of yourself.

God loves you . . . in spite of yourself.

I waited patiently for the Lord;
He turned to me and heard my cry.
He lifted me out of the slimy pit,
out of the mud and mire;
He set my feet on a rock
and gave me a firm place to stand.
He put a new song in my mouth,
a hymn of praise to our God.

Psalm 40:1–3

Chapter 13

Ready to Begin Anew

O Lord, You have searched me
*   and You know me.*
You know when I sit and when I rise;
*   You perceive my thoughts from afar.*
You discern my going out
*   and my lying down;*
*   You are familiar with all my ways.*
Before a word is on my tongue,
*   You know it completely, O Lord.*
You hem me in—behind and before;
*   You have laid Your hand upon me.*
Such knowledge is too wonderful for me,
*   too lofty for me to attain.*
*   Psalm 139:1–6*

God knows you far better than you know yourself. He has
been with you through it all—He knew how you'd feel and
react before you did. And He knew you would change. He
knew the day would come when you would stop rereading
Volume One of your life and would begin exploring Volume
Two.

And it would be a day of freedom—a day of victorious
elation. If your heart flipped long ago when you first felt love
for your mate, it now will burst with joy as that love flees.
It's like an iron cage opened—you're no longer a prisoner to
it—the "new you" can step out. You may already be separated
or divorced, but *now* you are free. There is no emotion left
. . . and you are anxious to begin a new life.

No emotion ...
> Save the urgency to be done!
> To have it finished!
> To be free!
> To meet the adventures of life.
> To start anew,
>   having learned.
> To enjoy all.
> To take each gift
>   and savor its peculiarity.
> To grab the future!
> To take each minute
>   and make all meaningful.
> To give myself!
> To ask for nothing
>   and find everything
>   in nothing.
> To seek God's plan!
> To find myself,
> To be myself!
> To use my gifts,
> To drain my resources.
> To flee to life!
> To grasp it gratefully,
> To sing its praises,
> To laud its blessings.

No emotion ... save Urgency!

One of the first things you must do to begin the new life is to get a new image of yourself. You've lived with a sense of failure far too long; it's time to discard it! Society has, by and large, measured your success as a wife by how well you've pleased your husband. And if the husband no longer wants her, a wife immediately supposes she has failed as a woman—as a person—and something is intrinsically wrong.

Now you must begin looking at yourself with new hope ... no, not just with hope, but with new confidence. The

78

process of healing puts the odds in favor of a new, fulfilling life. But *you* can't stand in the way. You can't put up obstacles that prevent new growth—obstacles such as clinging to the past with its hurts and disappointments, as seeking revenge for supposed wrongs, as giving up or lacking zest for new ventures.

It is true that you had to work out your grief slowly . . . with tears and talk and time. But that is ninety-nine percent over now, and you are ready to begin anew. Now you can look in the mirror and see someone you like, not dislike. Now you can have the courage to go out and do something you've always wanted to do, but were afraid to try. Now you can experience a rejuvenating intoxication with life and with yourself that will make you more self-assured than you've ever been. There can be times when you feel so self-confident that you'd like to talk with kings and entertain queens. The whole world is a challenge and few feats feared.

And this new you, as it blossoms and develops, will attract others. If the new strength is not built on vanity or loveless-ness, people will enjoy your company. You will again be a person worth liking . . . and if you're fortunate, worth loving.

> The joy of being loved!
>> Is there anything greater?
> To love
>> and know it brings response.
> To know the security
>> that it will endure through
>> the impossible,
>> and is yours to accept fully
>> if all else fails.
> A love that's free,
>> that exists no matter
>> what your choice.
> That respects your confusion,
>> and self-doubt,
> and responsibilities.

> That can live without
> > immediate fulfillment.
> That says—you are free,
> > do as you must . . .
> > I am here.

Whether you have new love or not, you can become anything you want to become. You can come out of this in better shape than you went into it—stronger, more poised, more confident of yourself than ever. You can do it, but you have to make the effort. You can't just sit back and do nothing. You must *ask* for change. It will be given to you (Matthew 7:7).

And you must begin *working* for the change. In order to make a new beginning, you must first of all understand yourself . . . you must have insight into what makes you tick.

One way to find out is to keep a notebook for yourself, or really of your reactions to everyday happenings. If something bothers you during the day, write down what it is. Then write down where it happened, what you were doing at the time, how you felt just before it happened, and any other such detail. Make a note of how your feelings were hurt, or what frustrated you, or what pressured you, and the like. Note also who were the party or parties involved. Follow the same procedure with happy incidents each day. Record not merely each joyous incident, but what happened before and after it.

After a month or so, read your "account book." You'll be surprised to find a pattern—a list of conditions, activities, and people who are good and bad medicine for you. Then use this insight to embrace what is good for you and to avoid what is bad.

Remember that this is your life, not someone else's. Don't let others make you over into their images. Don't let others decide what is right for you on the basis of what is right for them. If you remarry someday, still stay yourself. Never become a mere reflection of your new mate, unless this is what the real you wants.

If you do not feel ready for marriage, don't rush into it. Instead live through this period of new beginnings without making a commitment. Be sure of yourself; enjoy your life now. There will always be a tomorrow; do not push before you are ready. But do not close your mind to it.... There may be something even better in the future.

Listen
To your bells now
Pealing
    carefree color
Ringing
    sweeping freedom
The great golden
Bells

Listen to them now
The sound travels
And is
Gone
Time effaces
The enchanting melody
Of even an
Echo

Someday
You'll stand
Right under the bells
Looking up at a
Tarnished
Trim

Then
When your bells
Have a
Haunting hollow
Ring
    Consider
My

Warm wedding
Ring

You don't know what the future will bring. It may be that the present which you find so interesting today will pale tomorrow. You may wish to enjoy it for still a while. Yet you wonder . . . perhaps God has already opened tomorrow's door for you.

Yesterday
I was following a convertable
On the expressway,
And as my car
Sweeped and swooped,
I remembered
The swift sweet
Skylarks . . .

Today,
In an alley,
I passed a school door
And heard a bell,
Again I remembered . . .

Tomorrow
Perhaps I'll see
A heavy black coat,
Or hear the Psalms
Chanted,
Or smell
Red red roses,
Or taste dry
White wine,
And I'll remember . . .
I'll remember . . .

Your future's up to you . . . and yet not you alone. Don't try to change yourself without God's help. Don't begin a new life that doesn't center on Him. Ask yourself what alternatives there are for lifelong fulfillment and satisfaction. Look at the neighbor next door, the worker at the next desk. Ask if the endless cleaning, for example, or double workweeks work. Check if meaningless chatter or continual kaffee klatches console. See if the extended social life or daily pills bring any lasting bubbles. Question whether reading your daily horoscope results in any reliable answers or inner peace. Inspect all the alternatives you can and then compare them to the One who says: "Peace I leave with you; My peace I give you. I do not give to you as the world gives" (John 14:27).

If you have slipped and fallen, get up and walk back. Change *with* your Lord, not without Him. For it is He who came that all "may have life, and have it to the fullest" (John 10:10). That life isn't just a "You and me, God" proposition. It isn't something you mediate about now and then as you ride a commuter train or work in your garden. It's being alive and active within His people—or staying dead and dormant without. The blessings you reap will be in ratio to the interest you sow. So find the congregation that is most like home for you. Make it your family in Christ, eat at its table, and rejoice in its home. For "if anyone is in Christ, he is a new creation" (2 Corinthians 5:17).

> *How can I repay the Lord*
> *for all His goodness to me?*
> *I will lift up the cup of salvation*
> *and call on the name of the Lord.*
> *I will fulfill my vows to the Lord*
> *in the presence of all His people. . . .*
> *Praise the Lord!*
> *Psalm 116:12–14, 19*

Chapter 14

New Life

God has surely listened
 and heard my voice in prayer.
Praise be to God,
 who has not rejected my prayer,
 or withheld His love from me!
   Psalm 66:19–20

Therefore my heart is glad,
 and my tongue rejoices;
 my body also will rest secure . . . .
You have made known to me the path of life;
 You will fill me with joy in Your
presence,
 with eternal pleasures at Your right hand.
   Psalm 16:9, 11

In many ways life seems its old self again. Your children, yelling from your window to a neighbor's, sound very much like children all over the world. Their singsong, calling voices remind you of yours as a child.

> Hey Scaaa
> deee . . .
>
> Canya come owww
> ttt?
> Ask your maaa
> ther!
>
> Nooo, let's play
> herrre . . .
>
> I donwanna . . .

come over myyy
house . . .

No, I
won't

I donlikeyu
either!

Comaww
nnn . . .

Pleezzz . . .

Everybody says you're the way you used to be. You know
you're not. You know you will never be the same person
again. You've lived too much. You've changed. But now you
know what your friends mean. You're healthy and whole, and
the future can only get better. You'll always respect the experience you had. It was hell . . . and yet a cleansing by fire.
It was a humbling healing and has made you more aware and
understanding of others' problems and weaknesses.

The period has passed when your means of coping were
extreme—totally immersing yourself in your work or in your
children or in your leisure life. When you turn to new activities now, it is not because they are means of escape, but
because you enjoy them and they express the new you. Now
you're really getting something out of those evening classes
you attend; cooking is once more a joy; tennis has become a
refreshing sport; and your social activities are now a matter
of choice rather than need.

You're even thinking of remarriage again. Oh, maybe not
yet, but at least you no longer say you'll *never* remarry! You're
surprised at the lack of understanding some close friends and
relatives have when you indicate you may cast off your som-
ber mourning cloak and trade it in for a coat of many colors.
The possibilities before you in life are numerous, and you are
now ready to start investigating them.

For two years
I walked a tightrope . . .
A long slender rope
That led nowhere . . .

And nowhere was still . . .
And endless . . .
And the rope, slack.
Everyone smiled
And scattered nets
Yelling bravo!

And now
It's a rope
Tight
With short jets
To the
EVERYWHERE
near!

For some time your youngest children have been asking each new date, "Are you going to be my new daddy?" It has proven embarrassing at times and humorous at others. But the youngsters mean it. It is not uncommon for children to *want* two parents in the home. They may even tell you to go out and find a husband. Older children may have more reservations. And of course there are some youngsters who are just out-and-out against the whole idea. But children who feel loved by you will not be threatened.

There are various reasons why you may consider giving up even a fascinating, richly blessed single life to reenter the state of matrimony. You may miss the home life you once knew—with a husband who played with the children, laughed with you in the kitchen and helped with the cooking, made your dwelling feel "warm" rather than empty and lonely. You may miss the day-by-day companionship of someone who really cares and is truly interested in even the little things that make up your world. You may miss having someone to share the children's accomplishments and to help you in raising them. You may wish to give your children a "complete" home with two live-in parents. You may miss the sexual fulfillment and joy that can be found in a good marriage. You may wish to resume the role of wife which you truly loved.

Love is still the major reason for remarrying. And divorced people by and large are marrying people. It is possible to learn from one's past.

Even if you had few complaints regarding your former union, you may find that the new marriage is a brilliant gem— as different from the old as champagne is from beer. The beer may have gone flat, but the champagne bubbles can last *if* . . . *if* you do not marry the same type of person you did before (though there are some exceptions to this "if"); *if* you know who you are and can evaluate your strengths and faults realistically; *if* you and your new husband make God the most important part of your lives; *if* you always keep the lines of communication open between you; *if* you continue to respect each other as individual persons rather than role-players of your own making; *if* you keep faithful to each other while faithful to yourselves.

> Free   free   free
>
> Independently
> Free
> And yet one
> With you . . .
>
> What a phenomenon!
> I'm me,
> And you and me,
> And part of you,
> And yet me.
>
> See how love
> Does
> Freely bind:
> A mysterious

> One but two,
> Or is it
> Two but one?
> Until two are,
> They can never know
> The blessed state.
> > Little wonder
> > > God can be Triune ...

It is a common fallacy, however, to judge a divorced woman's rehabilitation in terms of whether she has successfully remarried. Marriage is not for everyone, nor should all people be expected to fulfill themselves in the same way. Many a divorced women feels that remaining single is not as dreadful as society—married society, that is—would have them believe. They know it is possible for a person to lead a joyous, fulfilling life as *either* a single or married person.

The God who is Love gives us love in many, many ways. He offers us all gifts, if we but open our hearts and accept them. He tells us to look around and see all the manifestations of His blessings.

Life *can* be beautiful! It *can* be a thing of beauty—a joy forever. There are so many blessings available in life that we cannot comprehend them all. And there is no way we can fully appreciate God or the gifts He has in store for us.

> Oh, the depth of the riches of the wisdom
> > and knowledge of God!
> How unsearchable His judgments,
> > and paths beyond tracing out!
> "Who has known the mind of the Lord?
> > Or who has been His counselor?"
> "Who has ever given to God,
> > that God should repay him?"
> For from Him and through Him and
> > to Him are all things.
> To Him be the glory forever! Amen.
> > *Romans 11:33–36*

To God be all glory. It is God who has given us physical life and has upheld us when it was weak! It is God who has sent a Savior to save us from eternal death! It is God who has sent His Spirit to fill us with new life! God is the Alpha and the Omega—the beginning and the end of love and life. We can only respond to God and to His unmerited gifts with the shout of the psalmist!

> *Praise the Lord, O my soul;*
> *all my inmost being,*
> *praise His holy name.*
> *Praise the Lord, O my soul,*
> *and forget not all His benefits—*
> *who forgives all your sins*
> *and heals all your diseases,*
> *who redeems your life from the pit*
> *and crowns you with*
> *love and compassion,*
> *who satisfies your desires with good things*
> *so that your youth is*
> *renewed like the eagle's....*
> *Praise the Lord, O my soul!*
> *Psalm 103:1–5, 22*

Postscript

O Lord my God, I called to You for help
    and You healed me.
O Lord, You brought me up
      from the grave;
You spared me from going down
      into the pit.
Sing to the Lord, you saints of His;
    praise His holy name.
For His anger lasts only a moment,
    but His favor lasts a lifetime;
weeping may remain for a night,
    but rejoicing comes in the morning.
    Psalm 30:2–5

For a step-by-step guide through divorce recovery and getting on with your life, see *Life after Divorce*, Bobbie Reed, Ph. D., published by Concordia Publishing House, available at your Christian bookstore.

"I Don't Want to Be Divorced!"

Your first response to the idea of a divorce was probably the same as mine: *I don't want to be divorced!* Rejection is always a shock. Even if your marriage has been deteriorating for a long time, it is still hard to face the fact that it will end in a divorce. Most of us hope that things will get better. We hope in spite of the reality of what is happening. We hope when it no longer makes sense to hope. And then, we secretly hope even when all hope is gone! We don't want to admit that our marriage has failed.

The one person you care most about in your life has just walked out. You feel that you have lost the only thing of value to you, a love relationship with your mate. You are in shock. You are numb. There is no strong emotional response because you are immobilized. The shock response actually provides a little of the emotional space and padding that you will need when you first face the possibility of a divorce. When Janine's husband told her he wanted a divorce, she looked at him blankly, then asked him what he wanted for supper that night. Nothing was registering because she was in shock. She couldn't understand or accept what was going on, so she rejected the idea.

The shock initally leads to denial that this is happening to you. You have a vague sense that if you just stand still, it won't happen. You can't take it all in. Your mind is rejecting the idea. This can't be happening, you tell yourself. It is all a cruel joke. This is just a temporary, crazy notion. He/she will be back. If you are in denial, you may fall into one or more of these behavior patterns:

- Perry tried to keep his life going as normally as possible. He did the laundry, cooked the meals, went to work, took care of the car, went out with friends, and never mentioned the fact that his spouse had moved out or discussed the possibility of divorce.
- Coral pulled away from her friends and her spouse, as well as her job, in an attempt to distance herself from people who might know what was going on. In that way, she could refuse to face the facts.
- Harold intensified his spiritual activities (reading the Bible, going

to church, praying) to see if God would make his spouse abandon the idea of divorce.

- Jim filled his life with lots of new and different tasks to keep him from thinking about the idea of a divorce. Suddenly, he had the energy to complete all of the unfinished projects he had ignored for the last 10 years.
- Phyllis began spending time with her in-laws to reassure herself that the family configuration was not going to change.
- Oliver tried to bargain with his spouse to keep her from leaving. Suddenly, nothing was as important to him as keeping the marriage intact.

Denial Is Natural

As the initial shock wears off, it is natural to want to deny what is happening. It's too frightening to face the implications a divorce would have in your life.

Remember when you first fell in love? Wasn't it wonderful? Being in romantic love is like having a magic mirror in which we always appear beautiful, handsome, talented, strong, and terrific. People in love temporarily lose touch with reality, as they begin to live a fantasy existence. Suddenly all of the love songs are unbelievably true. The sky is bluer. The birds do sing sweetly. Eyes sparkle. Cheeks flush. Tender glances speak volumes. Life becomes an adventure for two. And, since so much of the fairy tale notions about love seem to be coming true, then it must also follow that the *living happily ever after part* will be true.

As time passes, married couples realize that life together is not *always* wonderful; yet a part of us tries to hang onto the fairy tale. In the fairy tale there is no place for divorce. You may find that you are clinging to your spouse at this stage of the process, more from a reluctance to lose the fairy tale than because you don't want to live without that person. Uppermost in your mind is the question of how to get your loved one to return and to resume the marriage. You don't want another love, not even a better one. In fact, if you genuinely believe that there is no hope for a reconciliation, you might not even want to live.

But live you must! God is watching over you. Ps. 56:8 says that God catches your tears in a bottle and records them in His book. 1 Peter 5:7 tells us to cast all our cares on Him, because He loves us. Don't give up faith at this point. God will never give up on you.